MATH MASTERS ANALYZE THIS!

Dots, Plots, and Histograms

Claire Piddock

Rourke
Educational Media

rourkeeducationalmedia.com

Scan for Related Titles and
Teacher Resources

Before Reading:

Building Academic Vocabulary and Background Knowledge

Before reading a book, it is important to tap into what your child or students already know about the topic. This will help them develop their vocabulary, increase their reading comprehension, and make connections across the curriculum.

1. *Look at the cover of the book. What will this book be about?*
2. *What do you already know about the topic?*
3. *Let's study the Table of Contents. What will you learn about in the book's chapters?*
4. *What would you like to learn about this topic? Do you think you might learn about it from this book? Why or why not?*
5. *Use a reading journal to write about your knowledge of this topic. Record what you already know about the topic and what you hope to learn about the topic.*
6. *Read the book.*
7. *In your reading journal, record what you learned about the topic and your response to the book.*
8. *After reading the book complete the activities below.*

Content Area Vocabulary
Read the list. What do these words mean?

categorical
data
deviation
frequency
interquartile range
interval
mean absolute deviation
numerical
statistics
variability

After Reading:

Comprehension and Extension Activity

After reading the book, work on the following questions with your child or students in order to check their level of reading comprehension and content mastery.

1. *What do a histogram and a bar graph have in common?* (Summarize)
2. *Can a bar graph and a pictograph show the same data?* (Infer)
3. *What is one way to organize categorical data?* (Asking questions)
4. *What is the advantage of using a box plot to analyze and organize data?* (Text to self connection)
5. *What does the interquartile range tell you?* (Asking questions)

Extension Activity

Practice all the concepts in the book to master dots, plots, and histograms!

Table of Contents

What is Data?

You get statistical **data** when you ask questions that have more than one answer. The data are numbers that you can analyze. You count the different answers and get numbers that you can analyze. You can get data when you count the answers to questions.

Students might choose corn, carrots, or peppers as their favorite vegetable in a class survey. Suppose each picture is a vote for that vegetable.

Each vote is a data value. Count them.

There are 20 votes or 20 data values. Organize the data by counting the number of votes for each vegetable.

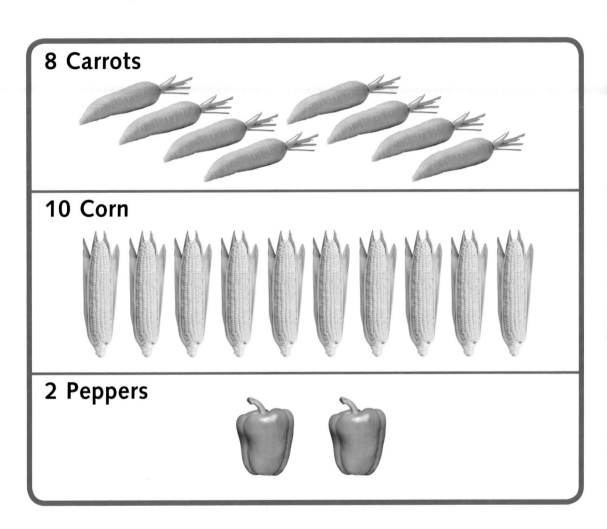

8 Carrots

10 Corn

2 Peppers

Statistics are all about the questions you ask, the kind of answers you can get, how you organize the answers, and how you display and understand those answers.

Pictographs

Our vegetable data are called **categorical** data. The categories are the different vegetable choices, and each choice (or vote) is one data value.

A pictograph is one way to organize categorical data. A pictograph has a key that tells what each symbol stands for.

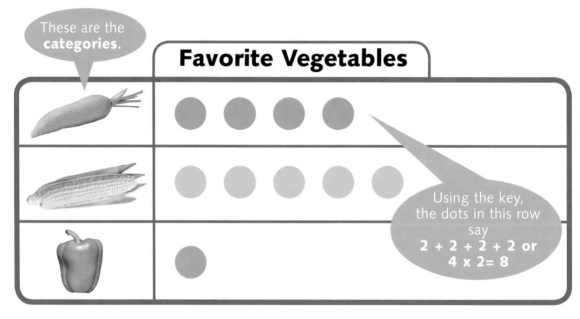

These are the **categories**.

Favorite Vegetables

Using the key, the dots in this row say
**2 + 2 + 2 + 2 or
4 x 2= 8**

Each ● stands for 2 votes.

In a pictograph, the key symbol can stand for 1, 2, 3, or any number of data values.

You can answer questions about students' vegetable preferences using the data in the pictograph.

- Which was the most popular vegetable?

Corn because that choice has the most dots.

- How many students chose peppers?

2 students because 1 dot means that 2 students chose peppers.

- How many more students chose carrots than peppers?

6 more students: 8 chose carrots and 2 chose peppers. 8 − 2 = 6

Bar Graphs

A bar graph is another way to organize categorical data. This bar graph uses the same vegetable data.

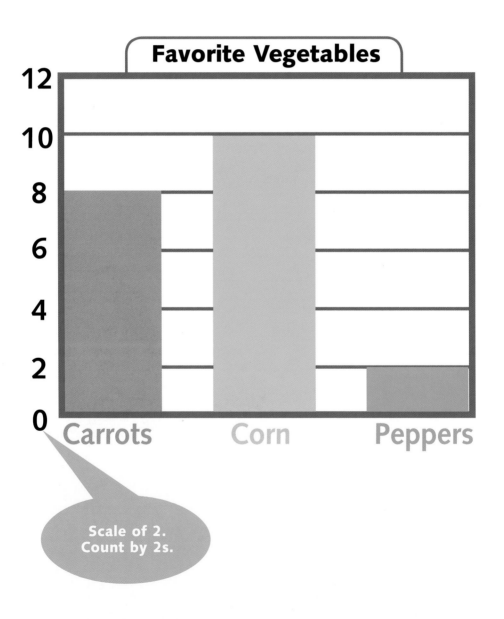

Favorite Vegetables

Scale of 2. Count by 2s.

The bar graph also shows that

8 people chose carrots.
10 people chose corn.
2 people chose peppers.

Here are some more questions you can answer.

a. How many students in all chose corn and peppers?

b. What was the most frequent answer?

c. What was the difference between the greatest number and least number in the data?

The most frequent number is the mode. When there is a tie, you have more than one mode. The difference between the greatest and least numbers is the range.

Dot Plots

We get **numerical** data from measurements such as the number of inches or the number of minutes.

Let's say students in a science class measured the height of their bean plants, which were all planted at the same time. Each measurement is a data value that can be organized in a chart. Make a mark called a tally for each plant's height. The number of tallies for each height is called the **frequency**.

Height of Bean Plants		
Height	**Tally**	**Frequency**
3	$\|\|$	2
$3\frac{1}{2}$	$\|\|\|$	3
4	$\|$	1
$4\frac{1}{2}$	$\|\|\|\|$	4

A dot plot is a way to display numerical data. Each tally will be 1 dot on the dot plot.

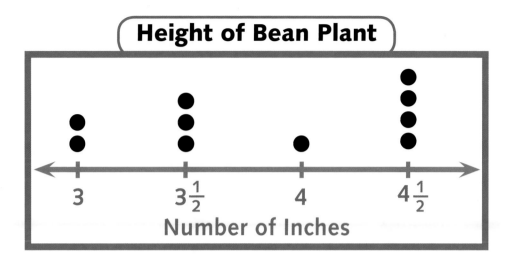

Height of Bean Plant

Number of Inches

A dot plot helps you answer these questions:

• How many plants were 4 inches tall?

1 because there is 1 dot above the 4 on the number line.

• How many students measured their bean plants?

10 students because there are 10 dots.

• How many plants were less than 4 inches tall?

5; There are 2 dots above the 3 and 3 dots above $3\frac{1}{2}$. 2 + 3 = 5

• How many plants were more than 4 inches tall? 4

Here is a dot plot about a type of grasshopper called a katydid.

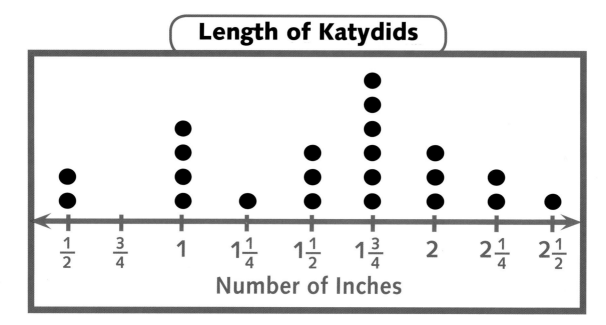

Length of Katydids

Number of Inches

You can answer addition and subtraction questions.

• What is the difference in length between longest and the shortest katydids?

• If the smallest katydids sat end to end, how long would they be together?

Answers: $2\frac{1}{2} - \frac{2}{2} = 2$

$\frac{1}{2} + \frac{1}{2} = 1$ inch

• If you saw a katydid that was $\frac{3}{4}$ inch longer than the shortest katydid in the dot plot, how many inches long would it be?

To add $\frac{1}{2} + \frac{3}{4}$ you need a common denominator.

$\frac{1}{2} = \frac{2}{4}$. So $\frac{1}{2} + \frac{3}{4} = \frac{2}{4} + \frac{3}{4}$

$$= \frac{5}{4} \text{ or } 1\frac{1}{4} \text{ inches}$$

Some people say this bug got its common name from its sound "katydid katydidn't". Its scientific category is *Tettigoniidae*.

Analyzing Data

When you analyze data, you look at measures that help you understand the data, A measure of center is a value at the center or middle of a data set.

The median is a measure of center. It tells you the middle value. Half of the data values are above the median and half the data values are below the median.

Let's say you download 8 songs to your device. The length of the songs in minutes are **2, 5, 8, 4, 5, 5, 2, 5**.

You can find the median by looking at the ordered list of values. If you write the data values in order from least to greatest, you have **2, 2, 4, 5, 5, 5, 5, 8**.

The middle value is between the 4th and 5th data value. Easy—the middle between 5 and 5 is 5. **Median = 5 minutes**

You can make this dot plot to show the lengths of your song downloads.

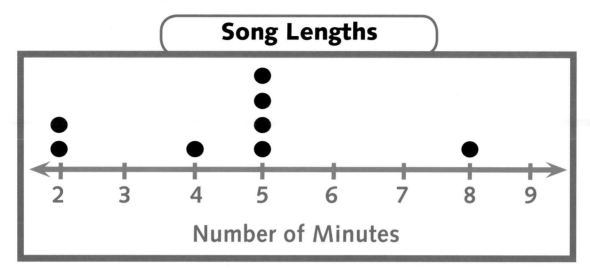

Song Lengths

Number of Minutes

You can find the median directly from the dot plot by looking for the middle dot. The middle value is between the 4th and 5th dot.

Median = 5 minutes

The mean is another measure of center. It is the average data value. To find the mean, add the number of minutes and divide by the number of data values.

Your data values were:

2, 2, 4, 5, 5, 5, 5, and 8

2 + 2 + 4 + 5 + 5 + 5 + 5 + 8 = 36

Then divide by 8 because there are 8 numbers or 8 data values.

Mean = 36 ÷ 8 = $4\frac{1}{2}$ minutes

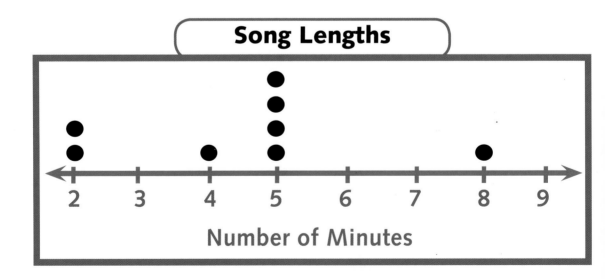

Song Lengths

Number of Minutes

You can use the dot plot to find the mean this way.

2 dots with value of 2: 2 x 2 = 4
1 dot with value of 4:   1 x 4 = 4
4 dots with value of 5: 4 x 5 = 20
1 dot with value of 8:   1 x 8 = 8

$4 + 4 + 20 + 8 = 36$ $36 ÷ 8 = 4\frac{1}{2}$ **minutes**

Mean = $4\frac{1}{2}$ **minutes**

There are more ways to analyze a dot plot.
Do you see how some values are separated from the others? These are called outliers.

a. What are the outliers in this dot plot?

You can also describe the gaps. There are no dots or data values in the gaps. Usually, if there are gaps, you will also notice clusters, where data is bunched up together.

b. Where are the gaps in this dot plot?

Histograms

A histogram is like a bar graph because it shows the frequency or how many times the numbers occur.

This data shows the number of text messages 20 teenagers sent in a day.

22	57	9	33	18	29	66	62	55	59
75	68	25	35	59	65	47	70	78	67

In a histogram, the data are grouped together. Each group is called an **interval**. To organize the data into groups, look at the least and greatest numbers and choose a convenient interval.

The least number of texts is 9. The greatest number of texts is 78. Intervals of 10 between 0 and 79 give us 8 equal intervals that include all the data.

Make a frequency table by counting the number in each interval.

Interval	0-9	10-19	20-29	30-39	40-49	50-59	60-69	70-79
Frequency	1	1	3	2	1	4	5	3

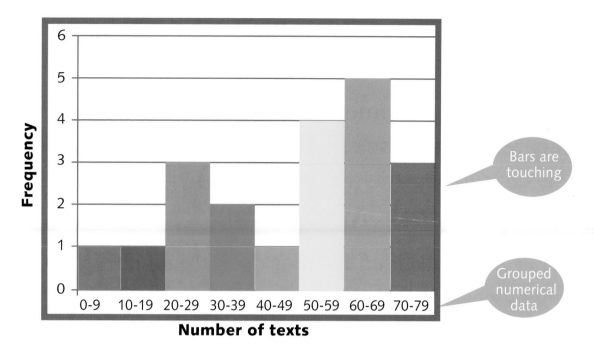

A histogram and a bar graph are different.
Here is a bar graph that shows the number of
texts made by five individual students. Compare it
with the histogram above.

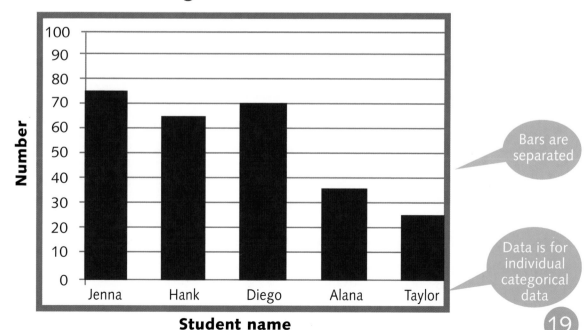

Box Plots

Box plots are another way to organize and analyze data. A box plot helps you visualize data by considering the median (middle value) and the spread or **variability** of the data.

These data resulted from asking 11 students how many cousins they have:

6, 3, 7, 8, 12, 5, 5, 4, 3, 4, 7

Step 1: Arrange the data values in order.

3, 3, 4, 4, 5, ⑤, 6, 7, 7, 8, 12

Step 2: Find the median. The middle number is ⑤
You have divided the data in half.

Step 3: Now find the median of each half.

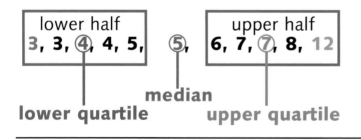

You've divided the data into 4 parts or fourths. These parts are called quartiles.

Step 4: Identify the extremes, the least and the greatest data value.

The **lower extreme** is **3**. The **upper extreme** is **12**.

With these 5 numbers, you can make a box plot.

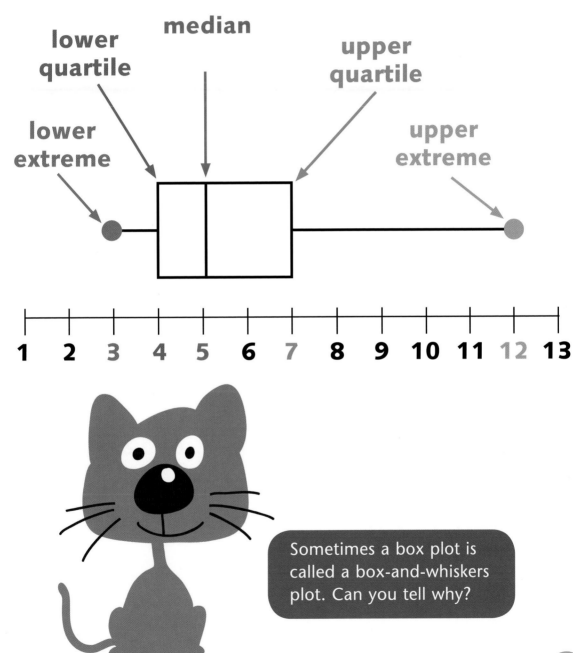

Sometimes a box plot is called a box-and-whiskers plot. Can you tell why?

Interquartile Range

Take another look at the box plot for the cousins' data.

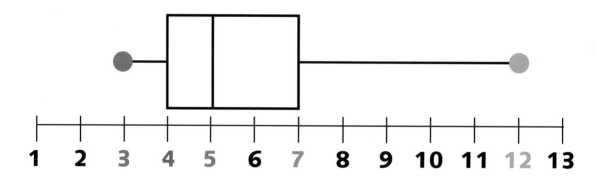

A measure called the **interquartile range**—IQR for short—gives you information about how spread out the data is.

Summary of what you know so far:

Data: 3, 3, 4, 4, 5, 5, 6, 7, 7, 8, 12
Median = 5
Upper quartile = 7
Lower quartile = 4
Lower extreme or least value = 3
Upper extreme or highest value = 12

The range of data is the difference between the highest and lowest values. **12 – 3 = 9**

The interquartile range is the difference between the upper quartile and the lower quartile.
IQR = **7 – 4 = 3**

The interquartile range tells you that 50% of the data values are between **4** and **7**.

• Now it's your turn. Look at this box plot.

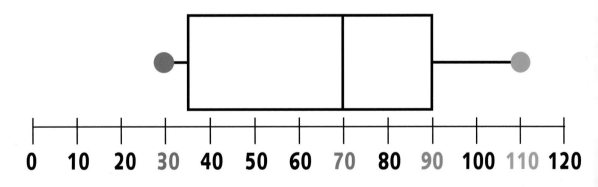

0 10 20 30 40 50 60 70 80 90 100 110 120

• Analyze the box plot.

a. What is the median?
b. What is the range?
c. What is the IQR?

c. 90 − 35 = 55
b. 110 − 30=80
a. 70

Mean Absolute Deviation

The **mean absolute deviation**—or MAD for short —is another way to look at how spread out (or not spread out) data is. It is based on finding the simple mean.

$$\textbf{Mean} = \frac{\text{sum of data values}}{\text{number of data values}}$$

Suppose this is data about the number of times in a year that some people went out to a movie:
7, 4, 17, 8, 12, 16, 9, 7

The mean is $\dfrac{4 + 7 + 7 + 8 + 9 + 12 + 16 + 17}{8} = \dfrac{80}{8} = \textbf{10}$

But that simple mean does not tell the whole story! We want to see, on the average, how far away from the mean the data values are.

Data values	Distance from 10
4	**10** – 4 = 6
7	**10** – 7 = 3
7	**10** – 7 = 3
8	**10** – 8 = 2
9	**10** – 9 = 1
12	12 – **10** = 2
16	16 – **10** = 6
17	17 – **10** = 7

Each green number is a **deviation** from the mean.

Now find the mean of these deviations:

$$\frac{6 + 3 + 3 + 2 + 1 + 2 + 6 + 7}{8} = \frac{30}{8} = \textbf{3.75}$$

The MAD is 3.75

Comparing Data

Compare box plots. The data are some student scores on two sample tests on state driving laws.

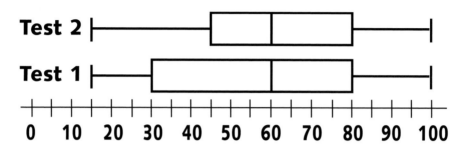

Here are some questions you can answer by looking at these box plots.

• What is the same about the two box plots?
The median is the same, 60. The highest and lowest scores are the same, so the range is the same.

• What is different about the box plots?
Results were more spread out in test 1 than in test 2. You can tell because the box is smaller for test 2.

• In general, did students do better on test 2?
Yes. You can tell by looking at the lower quartile that went up from 30 to 45 between the tests.

Compare dot plots. The data are the results of recording the number of hours a week that some students play video games and play sports.

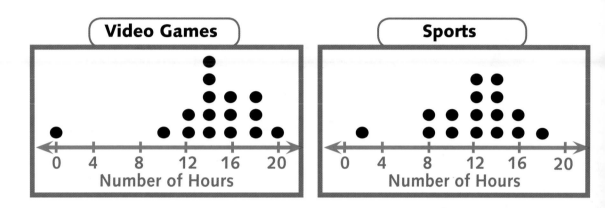

Here are some questions you can answer.

• What is the same about the two graphs? What is different?

They both have an outlier and a gap. There is a bigger gap in the video game data.

• In general, which activity did students spend the more time doing?

Playing video games.

• Which activity showed more variability?

Video game activity was more spread out.

Graph Type	Characteristics	Best Uses
Pictograph	Uses pictures that can represent one or more data values For categorical data, such as: • **favorite fruit** • **favorite color** • **eye color**	Small number of data values that can be expressed as multiples Easily compares different categories visually
Bar Graph	Uses vertical or horizontal bars For categorical data (see above)	Easily compare different categories visually
Dot Plot	Displays numerical data along a number line, such as: • **height** • **number of jumping jacks in 1 minute** Each dot represents one data value	Individual data values are shown, so better for small amount of data Shows general information such as **clusters, outliers, gaps**

Graph Type	Characteristics	Best Uses
Histogram	Does not show individual values; instead shows frequency data within equal intervals	Large amount of data
		Describing the general shape of data
	No gaps between bars Displays numerical data only, such as:	
	• **distances traveled to work** • **exam results for students**	
Box Plot	Does not show individual data values	Good visual summary based on 5 key numbers
	Displays the distribution of data based on 5 key numbers: median, minimum and maximum values (extremes); lower quartile, and upper quartile	Easy to compare characteristics of two or more different graphs
	Displays numerical data, such as: • **salaries for bank managers** • **length of airport delays**	

Glossary

categorical (kat-i-GAWR-i-kuhl): relating to divisions of people or things having particular shared characteristics

data (DAY-tuh): information collected in a place so that something can be done with it

deviation (dee-vee-AY-shun): the amount by which a single measurement differs from a fixed value such as the mean

frequency (FREE-kwuhnt-see): the number of times something happens

interquartile range (IQR) (IN-tur-KWUR-tile raynj): a measure of variability, based on dividing a data set into four equal parts called quartiles

interval (IN-tur-vuhl): a set of real numbers between two numbers either including or excluding one or both of them

mean absolute deviation (MAD) (meen AB-suh-LOOT dee-vee-AY-shun): in a set of data, the average distance between each data value and the mean

numerical (noo-MER-i-kuhl): relating to or expressed with numbers

statistics (stuh-TIS-tiks): the study of collected facts, measurements, or information for the purpose of analyzing, organizing, interpreting and presenting of data

variability (vair-ee-uh-BIL-it-tee): how much data values differ from each other

Index

Websites to Visit

www.education.com/worksheet/article/practice-test-
   bar-graphs-pictograms
www.commoncoresheets.com/LinePlots.php
www.mathsisfun.com/data/quartiles.htm

About The Author

Claire Piddock lives by a pond in the woods of Maine with her husband and big dog, Otto. She loves painting landscapes, doing puzzles, and reading mysteries. She sees math as a fun puzzle and enjoys taking the mystery out of math as she has done for many years as a teacher and writer.

Meet The Author!
www.meetREMauthors.com

www.rourkeeducationalmedia.com

PHOTO CREDITS: Cover: dots and graph © Allies Interactive, lightbulb "brain" © Positive Vectors; pages 4-5 carrot © Tarasyuk Igor, corn © bergamont, pepper © greatstockimages; page 6 speech bubble © FMStox, page 7 kid eating carrot © Nachaphon; page 13 katydid © Elliotte Rusty Harold; page 15 girl © PHILIPIMAGE; page 19 teens texting © Creativa Images; page 21 cat © krutikof; page 24 movie theater © Radu Bercan; page 29 © Rawpixel.com All images from Shutterstock.com

Edited by: Keli Sipperley

Cover and Interior design by: Nicola Stratford   www.nicolastratford.com

Library of Congress PCN Data

Dots, Plots, and Histograms / Claire Piddock
(Math Masters: Analyze This!)
ISBN 978-1-68191-737-5 (hard cover)
ISBN 978-1-68191-838-9 (soft cover)
ISBN 978-1-68191-931-7 (e-Book)
Library of Congress Control Number: 2016932661

Rourke Educational Media
Printed in the United States of America, North Mankato, Minnesota

Also Available as: